Monster Science

ALIENS
AND ENERGY

BY AGNIESZKA BISKUP · ILLUSTRATED BY AON

Consultant:
Philip Baringer, PhD
Department of Physics and Astronomy
University of Kansas

CAPSTONE PRESS
a capstone imprint

Graphic Library is published by Capstone Press,
151 Good Counsel Drive, P.O. Box 669, Mankato, Minnesota 56002.
www.capstonepub.com

Copyright © 2012 by Capstone Press, a Capstone imprint. All rights reserved.
No part of this publication may be reproduced in whole or in part, or stored in a
retrieval system, or transmitted in any form or by any means, electronic, mechanical,
photocopying, recording, or otherwise, without written permission of the publisher.
For information regarding permission, write to Capstone Press, 151 Good Counsel Drive,
P.O. Box 669, Dept. R, Mankato, Minnesota 56002.

Books published by Capstone Press are manufactured with paper
containing at least 10 percent post-consumer waste.

Library of Congress Cataloging-in-Publication Data
Biskup, Agnieszka.
Aliens and energy / by Agnieszka Biskup.
    p. cm.—(Graphic library. Monster science)
Includes bibliographical references and index.
Summary: "In cartoon format, uses aliens to explain the science of energy"—Provided by
publisher.
ISBN 978-1-4296-6580-3 (library binding)
ISBN 978-1-4296-7325-9 (paperback)
1. Force and energy—Juvenile literature. 2. Extraterrestrial beings—Juvenile literature.
3. Graphic novels. I. Title. II. Series.
QC73.4.B488 2012
530—dc22   2011004485

WITHDRAWN

Editor
Anthony Wacholtz

Art Director
Nathan Gassman

Designer
Lori Bye

Production Specialist
Eric Manske

Printed in the United States of America in Stevens Point, Wisconsin.
032011   006111WZF11

TABLE OF
CONTENTS

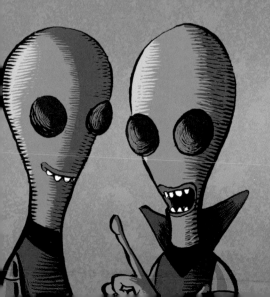

CHAPTER 1

ENERGY AND MATTER

Have you ever wondered how birds fly, fish swim, or aliens fly through space? Have you ever thought about why you can walk or run?

These are big questions with many answers. But a good place to start is with energy.

Energy makes everything happen in the universe. One way or another, you use energy in everything you do.

All living things need energy to move, grow, and change. But where do they get the energy? For many living things, food is the main source of energy.

WHAP!

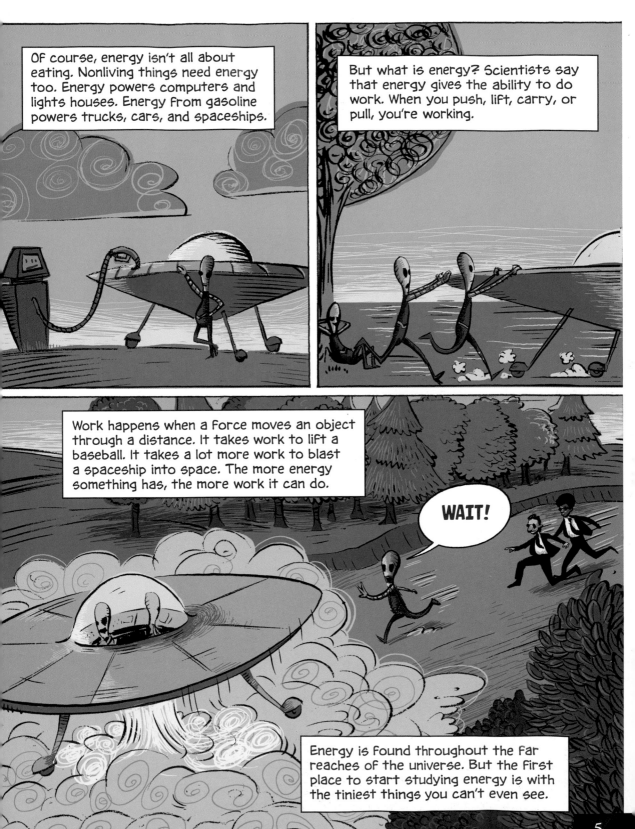

Of course, energy isn't all about eating. Nonliving things need energy too. Energy powers computers and lights houses. Energy from gasoline powers trucks, cars, and spaceships.

But what is energy? Scientists say that energy gives the ability to do work. When you push, lift, carry, or pull, you're working.

Work happens when a force moves an object through a distance. It takes work to lift a baseball. It takes a lot more work to blast a spaceship into space. The more energy something has, the more work it can do.

WAIT!

Energy is found throughout the far reaches of the universe. But the first place to start studying energy is with the tiniest things you can't even see.

To understand energy, you must first understand the stuff that makes up everything in the universe. That stuff is matter.

I HAVE A LOT OF MATTER.

Matter is anything that takes up space and has mass. Aliens, people, cars, and just about everything else is made of matter.

THAT CAR HAD MATTER.

Mass is the amount of material in an object. Consider a spaceship and an alien. Both are made of matter, but the spaceship has a lot more mass than the alien.

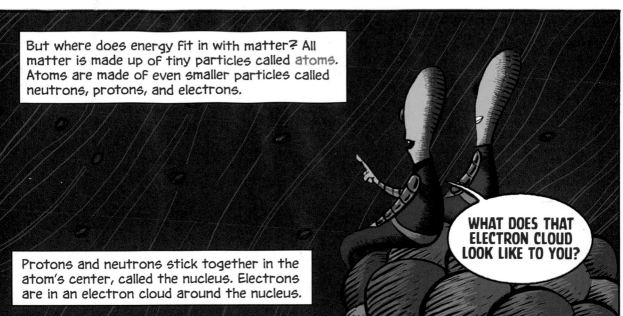

But where does energy fit in with matter? All matter is made up of tiny particles called atoms. Atoms are made of even smaller particles called neutrons, protons, and electrons.

WHAT DOES THAT ELECTRON CLOUD LOOK LIKE TO YOU?

Protons and neutrons stick together in the atom's center, called the nucleus. Electrons are in an electron cloud around the nucleus.

You can't see it, but atoms and molecules are never completely still. They're constantly vibrating. All that wiggling and jiggling produces energy.

MOLECULES

Atoms can join together to form groups called molecules. For example, one atom of oxygen and two atoms of hydrogen can combine to form a molecule of water. The atoms in a molecule are held together by energy.

atoms—tiny particles that are the basic building blocks of matter

CHAPTER 2

KINDS OF ENERGY

All the energy in the universe can be placed into two main groups—kinetic energy and potential energy. Kinetic energy is the energy of motion. Anything that moves has kinetic energy. Jiggling atoms, bouncing balls, and dancing aliens all have kinetic energy.

The faster something moves and the more mass it has, the more kinetic energy it has. A big alien has a lot more kinetic energy than a small alien when they run at the same speed.

Potential energy, on the other hand, is stored energy. A spaceship stuck high in a tree has potential energy.

If the spaceship crashes to the ground, its stored energy will be released in a spectacular way.

When you stretch a rubber band, you're storing energy as potential energy too.

If you let go of the stretched rubber band, the potential energy becomes kinetic energy.

kinetic energy—the energy of motion
potential energy—the stored energy of an object due to an object's position or what's been done to it

Whether it's kinetic or potential, there are many types of energy. One type is chemical energy. Chemical energy is the stored energy trapped in molecules.

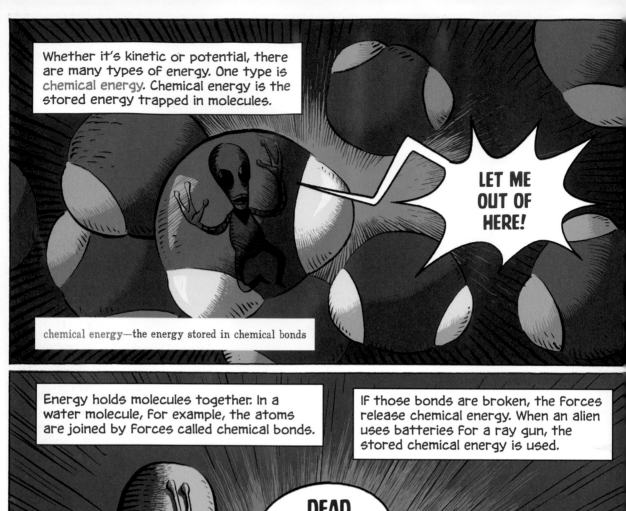

LET ME OUT OF HERE!

chemical energy—the energy stored in chemical bonds

Energy holds molecules together. In a water molecule, for example, the atoms are joined by forces called chemical bonds.

If those bonds are broken, the forces release chemical energy. When an alien uses batteries for a ray gun, the stored chemical energy is used.

DEAD BATTERIES AGAIN?!?

Food, gasoline, and other fuels also have chemical energy. People eat plants and animals to get energy. When you eat food, your body stores the chemical energy as fat and other substances.

But your muscles will use that stored chemical energy later. The stored energy changes into kinetic energy when you move.

HEY! YOU OWE ME $200!

Sound is another source of energy that's all around you. Music on the radio, the ticking of a clock, and the bang of a gong all have sound energy.

Sound is produced when the molecules and atoms in an object vibrate. The vibrations make the molecules and atoms hit each other.

The vibrations travel through the air as sound waves. You hear a sound when the vibrations reach your eardrum, causing it to vibrate too.

IN SPACE, NO ONE CAN HEAR YOU BURP

Sound waves need to travel through some kind of material, such as air, to make sound. Outer space is a vacuum, which means there is no air. So if you burped on the moon, no one would hear it.

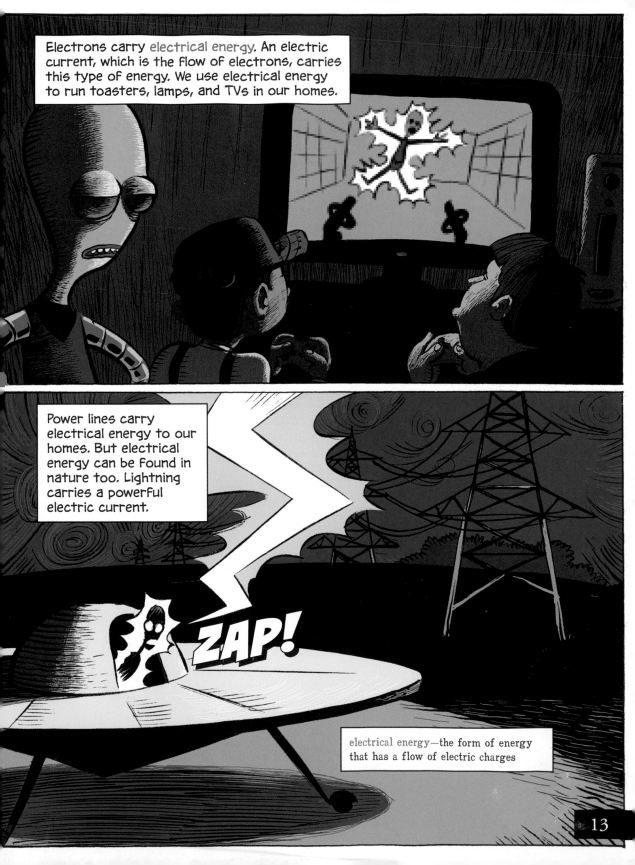

Electrons carry electrical energy. An electric current, which is the flow of electrons, carries this type of energy. We use electrical energy to run toasters, lamps, and TVs in our homes.

Power lines carry electrical energy to our homes. But electrical energy can be found in nature too. Lightning carries a powerful electric current.

ZAP!

electrical energy—the form of energy that has a flow of electric charges

13

We use electrical energy to light our homes, but light itself carries a form of energy. Light, like sound, travels in the form of waves.

Atoms create light when electrons move from higher to lower levels of energy. What we see as light is the energy that's given off from electrons jumping from one level to the other.

The light we see belongs to a family of waves called electromagnetic radiation. These waves can be separated into categories based on their wavelength.

DUDE, THAT COW IS FREAKING ME OUT!

This family includes gamma rays, X-rays, ultraviolet light, visible light, infrared light, microwaves, and radio waves.

14

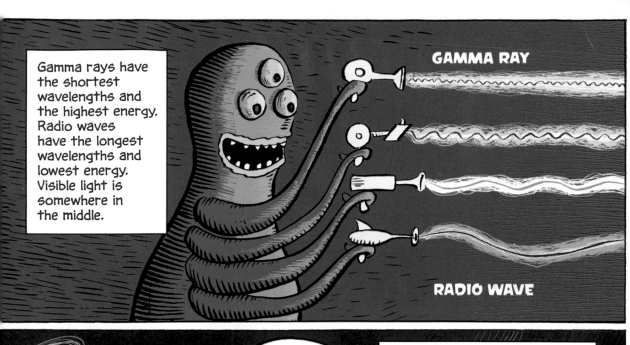

Gamma rays have the shortest wavelengths and the highest energy. Radio waves have the longest wavelengths and lowest energy. Visible light is somewhere in the middle.

GAMMA RAY

RADIO WAVE

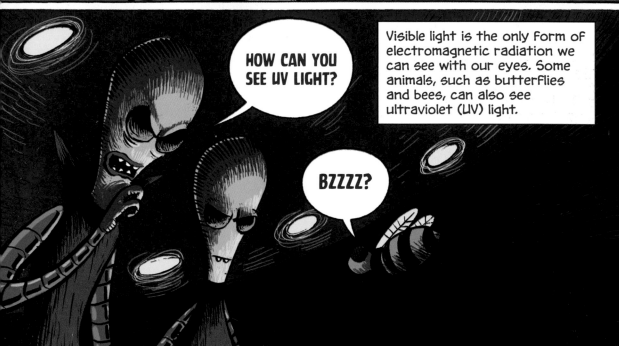

HOW CAN YOU SEE UV LIGHT?

BZZZZ?

Visible light is the only form of electromagnetic radiation we can see with our eyes. Some animals, such as butterflies and bees, can also see ultraviolet (UV) light.

SOUND VS. LIGHT

Sound waves move about 1,125 feet (343 meters) per second. That's fast! But nothing in the universe is faster than light. Light travels an amazing 186,000 miles (300,000 kilometers) per second. That's why you see lightning before you hear thunder.

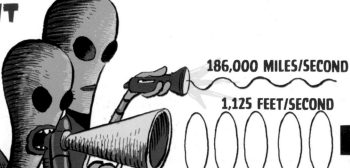

186,000 MILES/SECOND

1,125 FEET/SECOND

Another type of energy is heat. Atoms and molecules vibrating and moving around create heat, which is also known as thermal energy.

thermal energy—energy from the movement of atoms and molecules; also called heat energy

Atoms and molecules are always in motion. Because these particles are moving, they have kinetic energy.

Heat is the total amount of kinetic energy contained in an object's particles. The faster the atoms and molecules move, the hotter something is.

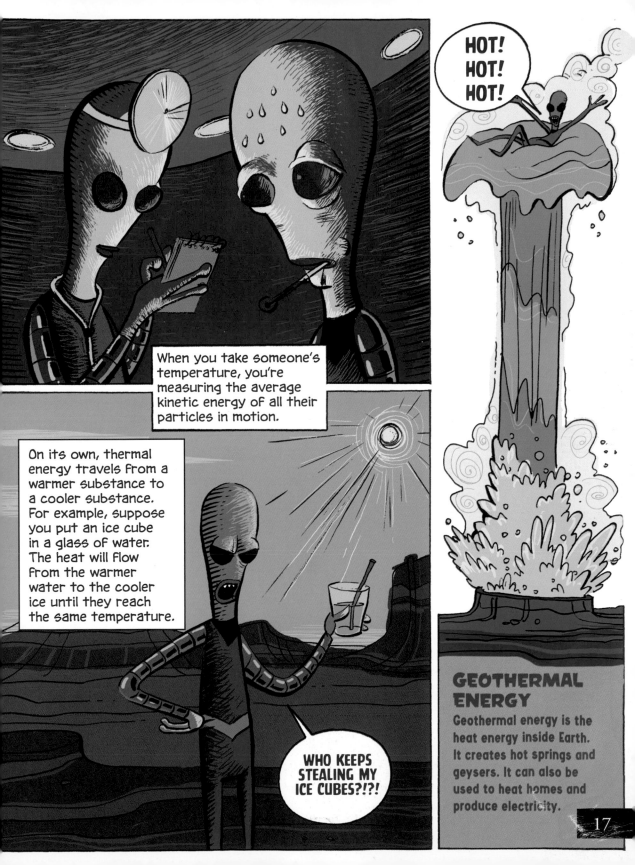

When you take someone's temperature, you're measuring the average kinetic energy of all their particles in motion.

On its own, thermal energy travels from a warmer substance to a cooler substance. For example, suppose you put an ice cube in a glass of water. The heat will flow from the warmer water to the cooler ice until they reach the same temperature.

HOT! HOT! HOT!

WHO KEEPS STEALING MY ICE CUBES?!?!

GEOTHERMAL ENERGY

Geothermal energy is the heat energy inside Earth. It creates hot springs and geysers. It can also be used to heat homes and produce electricity.

CHAPTER 3

CHANGING ENERGY

No matter what kind of energy we're talking about, it can't be created or destroyed. Energy can only be changed from one form to another. You can see this by setting a piece of wood on fire. Wood has stored chemical energy.

The chemical energy in the wood is transformed into heat energy, light energy, and even sound energy when the wood crackles.

Crackle!

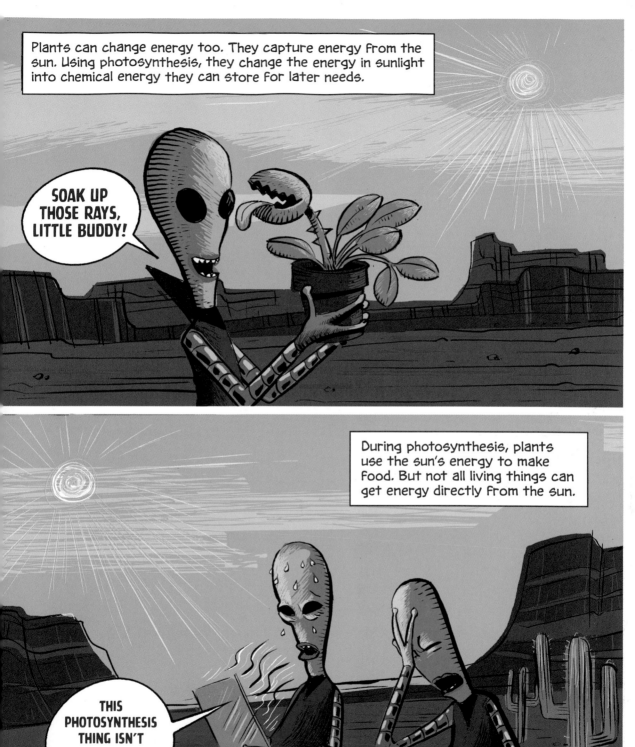

Plants can change energy too. They capture energy from the sun. Using photosynthesis, they change the energy in sunlight into chemical energy they can store for later needs.

SOAK UP THOSE RAYS, LITTLE BUDDY!

During photosynthesis, plants use the sun's energy to make food. But not all living things can get energy directly from the sun.

THIS PHOTOSYNTHESIS THING ISN'T WORKING. I'M STILL HUNGRY!

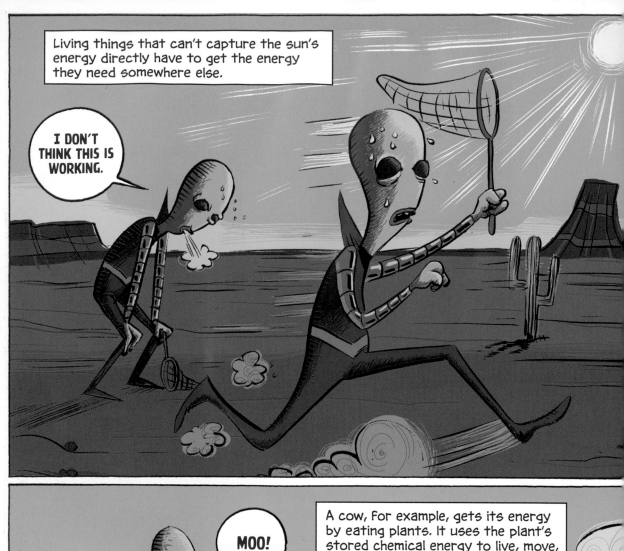

Living things that can't capture the sun's energy directly have to get the energy they need somewhere else.

I DON'T THINK THIS IS WORKING.

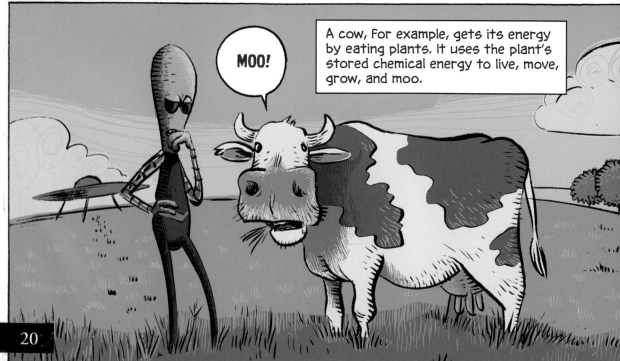

MOO!

A cow, for example, gets its energy by eating plants. It uses the plant's stored chemical energy to live, move, grow, and moo.

By eating meat, you use an animal's chemical energy to live, move, and grow too. It also gives you the energy to moo—if you want to, anyway.

MOO?

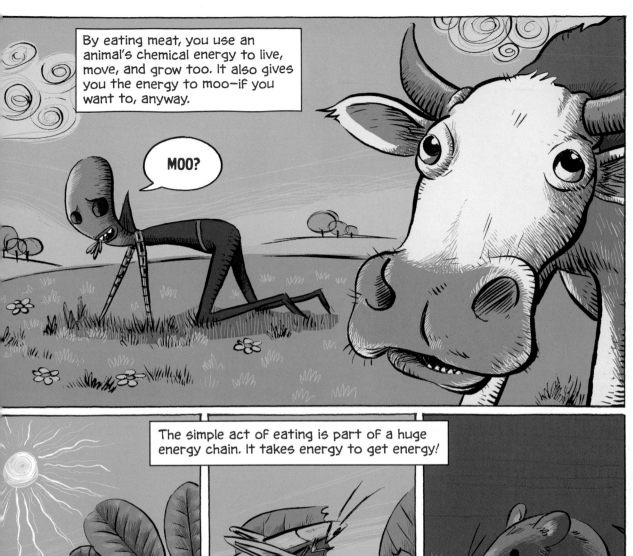

The simple act of eating is part of a huge energy chain. It takes energy to get energy!

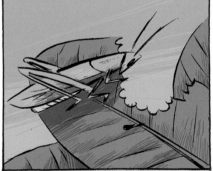

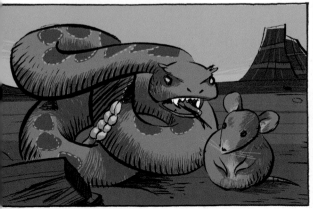

Slurp!

Everything in the universe is part of an energy chain. All things are connected through energy changing forms. Eating is an example of changing energy. So is turning on a flashlight or a lightbulb.

A flashlight changes stored chemical energy in its batteries into electrical energy. Some of the electrical energy is transferred as light energy when it is turned on.

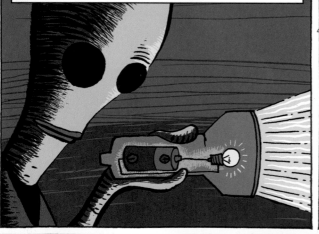

BOOOM!

When a firework explodes, the chemical energy stored within it gets transformed into heat energy, sound energy, and kinetic energy.

But even though energy can change form, it can never be destroyed. This is called the law of conservation of energy. The total amount of energy in each energy chain remains the same.

HE'S CONSERVING ENERGY, ALL RIGHT.

ZZZZZZ

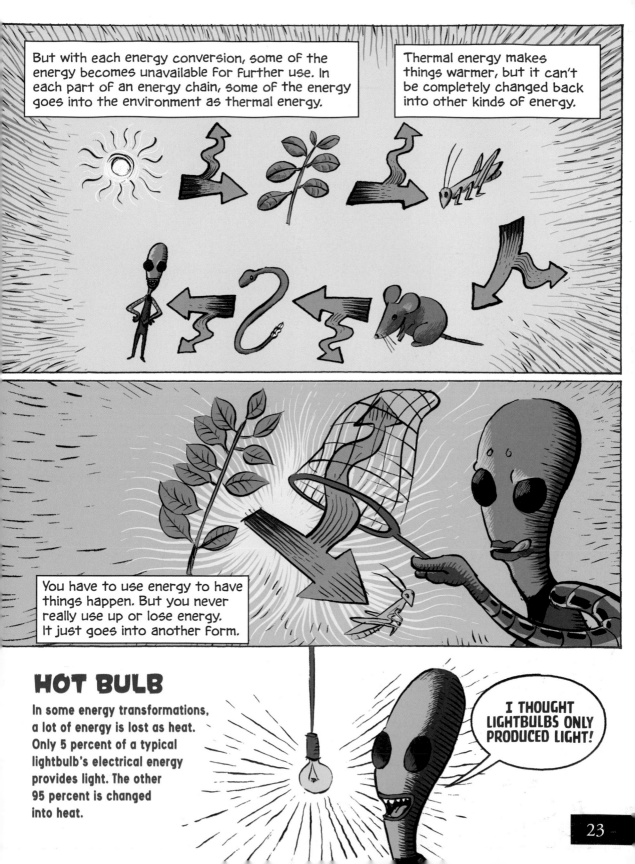

But with each energy conversion, some of the energy becomes unavailable for further use. In each part of an energy chain, some of the energy goes into the environment as thermal energy.

Thermal energy makes things warmer, but it can't be completely changed back into other kinds of energy.

You have to use energy to have things happen. But you never really use up or lose energy. It just goes into another form.

HOT BULB

In some energy transformations, a lot of energy is lost as heat. Only 5 percent of a typical lightbulb's electrical energy provides light. The other 95 percent is changed into heat.

I THOUGHT LIGHTBULBS ONLY PRODUCED LIGHT!

Even the energy we get from windmills and wind generators comes from the sun. Winds are created when the sun heats some parts of Earth more than others, which makes air move.

NUCLEAR ENERGY

Mass itself contains energy. The mass in the nucleus of atoms is the source of nuclear energy. There's a huge amount of energy holding the nucleus of an atom together. Nuclear energy is released when nuclei are broken apart or fused together. In nuclear power plants, energy is released when an atom's nucleus is split apart. In the sun, nuclear energy is produced when atomic nuclei are joined together.

YOU'RE NEVER GOING TO PULL THAT NUCLEUS APART.

TOO ... HEAVY ...

LOOKS LIKE HE'LL END UP AS A FOSSIL FUEL.

The sun is also the reason we have fossil fuels, such as oil, coal, and natural gas. Fossil fuels are formed from the ancient remains of plants and animals, which once used the sun for energy as well.

People depend on fossil fuels for energy. Most power plants burn fossil fuels for energy. For example, coal is burned to make electricity.

Burning coal heats water into steam. The high-pressure steam turns turbines, which drive generators to produce electricity. The electricity is then sent through electric lines to power communities and spaceships.

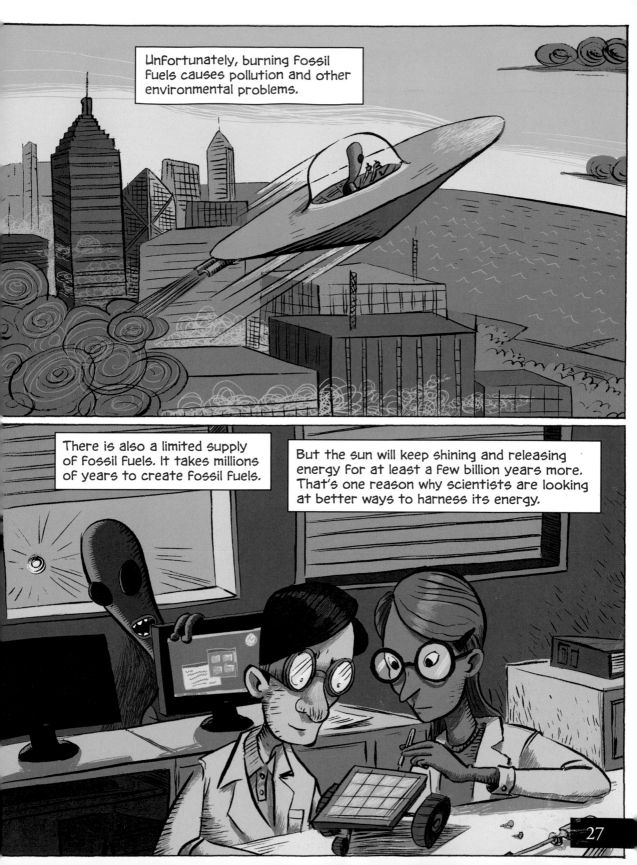

Unfortunately, burning fossil fuels causes pollution and other environmental problems.

There is also a limited supply of fossil fuels. It takes millions of years to create fossil fuels.

But the sun will keep shining and releasing energy for at least a few billion years more. That's one reason why scientists are looking at better ways to harness its energy.

It takes time to come up with efficient ways to use renewable sources of energy. That's why it's important to conserve energy where and when we can.

You're conserving energy each time you reuse or recycle paper, plastic, and metal.

GLASS

ALUMINUM

PAPER

SPACESHIPS

Using public transportation saves more energy than driving cars separately.

BUS STOP

Almost half of the energy used by Americans in their homes is used for space heating. Turning down the thermostat can help save energy.

Changing out inefficient lightbulbs with energy-efficient ones also helps save energy.

But there's a lot more to energy than saving fossil fuels. Energy is an important part of the universe. And life—alien or otherwise—couldn't exist without it.

GLOSSARY

atom (AT-uhm)—a tiny particle that is a basic building block of matter

chemical energy (KE-muh-kuhl EN-ur-jee)—the energy stored in chemical bonds

electrical energy (i-LEK-tri-kuhl EN-ur-jee)—the form of energy that has a flow of electric charges

kinetic energy (ki-NET-ik EN-ur-jee)—the energy of a moving object

molecule (MOL-uh-kyool)—a group of two or more atoms linked together

nuclear energy (NOO-klee-ur EN-ur-jee)—energy contained in the nucleus of an atom

potential energy (puh-TEN-shuhl EN-ur-jee)—the stored energy of an object

radiation (ray-dee-AY-shuhn)—a form of energy, such as heat, light, X-rays, microwaves or radio waves; radiation also includes dangerous, high-energy nuclear radiation

thermal energy (THUR-muhl EN-ur-jee)—energy from the movement of atoms and molecules; also called heat energy

wavelength (WAYV-length)—the distance between two peaks of a wave

READ MORE

Bailey, Gerry. *Out of Energy.* Planet SOS. New York: Gareth Stevens, 2011.

Drummond, Allan. *Energy Island.* New York: Farrar, Straus and Giroux, 2011.

Gosman, Gillian. *Earth-Friendly Energy.* How to Be Earth Friendly. New York: PowerKids Press, 2011.

INTERNET SITES

FactHound offers a safe, fun way to find Internet sites related to this book. All sites on FactHound have been researched by our staff.

Here's all you do:

Visit www.facthound.com

Type in this code: 9781429665803

Check out projects, games and lots more at
www.capstonekids.com

INDEX

31901051780817